A Gift of

Wesleyan University Press

APPLES FROM SHINAR

3 6
1 5

APPLES
FROM
SHINAR

A Book of Poems by

HYAM
PLUTZIK

WESLEYAN UNIVERSITY PRESS
MIDDLETOWN, CONNECTICUT

Grateful acknowledgment is made to the editors of the following publica-
tions in which some of these poems first appeared: *Accent, The American
Scholar, Antioch Review, Beloit Poetry Journal, Epoch, Fifteen Modern
American Poets* by George P. Elliott (Rinehart), *Furioso, The Hopkins
Review, New World Writing No. 8* (New American Library), *Prairie
Schooner, Saturday Review, The Sewanee Review, The Transatlantic
Review*, and *Yale Review*.

Library of Congress Catalog Card Number: 59–12479
Manufactured in the United States of America
First edition

TO THE MEMORY OF MY FATHER

CONTENTS

APPLES FROM SHINAR

Because the red osier dogwood
Is the winter lightning,
The retention of the prime fire
In the naked and forlorn season
When snow is winner
(For he flames quietly above the shivering mouse
In the moldy tunnel,
The eggs of the grasshopper awaiting metamorphosis
Into the lands of hay and the times of the daisy,
The snake contorted in the gravel,
His brain suspended in thought
Over an abyss that summer will fill with murmuring
And frogs make laughable: the cricket-haunted time)—
I, seeing in the still red branches
The stubborn, unflinching fire of that time,
Will not believe the horror at the door, the snow-white
        worm
Gnawing at the edges of the mind,
The hissing tree when the sleet falls.
For because the red osier dogwood
Is the winter sentinel,
I am certain of the return of the moth
(Who was not destroyed when an August flame licked
        him),
And the cabbage butterfly, and all the families
Whom the sun fathers, in the cauldron of his mercy.

This midnight dream whispered to me:
Be swift as a runner, take the lane
Into the green mystery
Beyond the farm and haystack at Stone.
You leave tomorrow, not to return.

Hands that were fastened in a vise,
A useless body, rooted feet,
While time like a bell thundered the loss,
Witnessed the closing of the gate.
Thus sleep and waking both betrayed.

I had one glimpse: In a close of shadow
There rose the form of a manor-house,
And in a corner a curtained window.
All was lost in a well of trees,
Yet I knew for certain this was the place.

If the hound of air, the ropes of shade,
And the gate between that is no gate,
Had not so held me and delayed
These cowardly limbs of bone and blood,
I would have met him as he lived!

Seventy-seven betrayers will stand by the road,
And those who love you will be few but stronger.

Seventy-seven betrayers, skilful and various,
But do not fear them: they are unimportant.

You must learn soon, soon, that despite Judas
The great betrayals are impersonal

(Though many would be Judas, having the will
And the capacity, but few the courage).

You must learn soon, soon, that even love
Can be no shield against the abstract demons:

Time, cold and fire, and the law of pain,
The law of things falling, and the law of forgetting.

The messengers, of faces and names known
Or of forms familiar, are innocent.

I AM DISQUIETED WHEN I
SEE MANY HILLS

I am disquieted when I see many hills,
As one who looks down on the backs of tremendous cattle,
Shoulder to shoulder, munching in silence the grass
    In a timeless region.

Where time is not, event and breath are nothing,
Yet we who are lost in time, growing and fading
In the shadow of majesty, cannot but dumbly yearn
    For its stronger oblivion.

Reject this archaic craving to be a herdsman
Of the immortals. Until they trample you down
Be still the herdsman's boy among these giants
    And the ridges of laurel.

As the great horse rots on the hill
  till the stars wink through his ribs;
As the genera of horses become silent,
  the thunder of the hooves receding in the silence;
As the tree shrivels in the wind of time,
  as the wind Time dries the locust tree—
Thus you prepare the future for me and my loved ones.

I have been in many towns and seen innumerable houses,
  also rocks, trees, people, stars and insects.
Thieves, like ants, are making off with them,
  taking them to your old ant-hill.
Thus you prepare the future for me and my loved ones.

What spider made the machine of many threads?

The threads run
  from time's instants to all the atoms of the universe.
In each instant a wheel turns in your head, threads go
   taut,
  and one of a quintillion atoms is transmuted.
Thus you prepare the future for me and my loved ones.

I observe the ordained explosions on the paper as I write,
The pinpoints of flame in the wood on the table, and on
   the wall
(Like a battlefield at night, or a field where fireflies
   flicker).
My hand, too, scintillates like a strange fish;
Fires punctuate the faces on the road;
A pox, a fever, burns in the tissues of the hills.
Thus you prepare the future for me and my loved ones.

As the great horse is transmuted on the hill
Till the stars wink through his skull;
As the stars become husk and radiance;
As the locust tree is changed by the wind Time;
As the wind Time too will lapse, will blow from another
        quarter—
Thus you prepare the future for me and my loved ones.

IF CAUSALITY IS IMPOSSIBLE, GENESIS IS RECURRENT

The abrupt appearance of a yellow flower
Out of the perfect nothing, is miraculous.
The sum of Being, being discontinuous,
Must presuppose a God-out-of-the-box
Who makes a primal garden of each garden.
There is no change, but only re-creation
One step ahead. As in the cinema
Upon the screen, all motion is illusory.
So if your mind were keener and could clinch
More than its flitting beachhead in the Permanent,
You'd see a twinkling world flashing and dying
Projected out of a tireless, winking Eye
Opening and closing in immensity—
Creating, with Its look, beside all else
Always Adamic passion and innocence,
The bloodred apple or the yellow flower.

No one cared for the iron sparrow
That fell from the sky that quiet day
With no bird's voice, a mad beast's bellow.

Sparrow, your wing was a broken scar
As you blundered into the mother-barley.
Sparrow, how many men did you bear?

"Ten good men, pilot and gunner—
Trapped in the whirlpool, held by no hands,
Twisting from truth with curse and prayer.

"Ten good men I bore in my belly—
Not as the mother-barley bears.
Ten good men I returned to her there."

Thunder rolling over the barley!
Fire swarming high and higher!

Home again to the barley-mother—
Ten good sons, pilot and gunner,
Radioman and bombardier.

Trying to imagine a poem of the future,
I saw a nameless jewel lying
Lurid on a table of black velvet.

Light winked there like eyes half-lidded,
Raying the dark with signals,
Lunar, mineral, maddening

As that white night-flower herself,
And with her delusive chastity.

Then one said: "I am the poet of the damned.
My eyes are seared with the darkness that you willed me.
This jewel is my heart, which I no longer need."

As I was fishing off Pondy Point
Between the tides, the sea so still—
Only a whisper against the boat—
No other sound but the scream of a gull,
I heard the voice you will never hear
Filling the crannies of the air.

The doors swung open, the little doors,
The door, the hatch within the brain,
And like the bellowing of ruin
The surf upon the thousand shores
Swept through me, and the thunder-noise
Of all the waves of all the seas.

The doors swung shut, the little doors,
The door, the hatch within the ear,
And I was fishing off Pondy Pier,
And all was as it was before,
With only the whisper of the swell
Against the boat, and the cry of a gull.

I draw a sight from tree to tree
Crossing this other from knoll to rock,
To mark the place. Into the sea
My line falls with an empty hook,
Yet fools the world. So day and night
I crouch upon the thwarts and wait.

There is a roaring in the skies
The great globes make, and there is the sound
Of all the atoms whirling round

That one can hear if one is wise—
Wiser than most—if one has heard
The doors, the little doors, swing wide.

AFTER LOOKING INTO A BOOK BELONGING TO MY GREAT-GRANDFATHER, ELI ELIAKIM PLUTZIK

I am troubled by the blank fields, the speechless graves.
Since the names were carved upon wood, there is no word
For the thousand years that shaped this scribbling fist
And the eyes staring at strange places and times
Beyond the veldt dragging to Poland.
Lovers of words make simple peace with death,
At last demanding, to close the door to the cold,
Only *Here lies someone.*
Here lie no one and no one, your fathers and mothers.

THE GEESE

A miscellaneous screaming that comes from nowhere
Raises the eyes at last to the moonward-flying
Squadron of wild-geese arcing the spatial cold.

Beyond the hunter's gun or the will's range
They press southward, toward the secret marshes
Where the appointed gunmen mark the crossing

Of flight and moment. There is no force stronger
(In the sweep of the monomaniac passion, time)
Than the will toward destiny, which is death.

Value the intermediate splendor of birds.

If I should round the corner quickly—
Or suddenly turn my head—
I know I'd catch them preparing the scene,
Painting a tree or hanging the moon,
Arranging houses and streets exactly
In the desperate game which is God's.

For I have seen through their plausible lies—
That of a uniform world,
And cities existing beyond these hills,
Or on rain-wet pampas ferocious bulls,
A logic of morrows and yesterdays
Or real seeds under this field.

The surface is thin as a gilding of oil
Upon an enormous lake
Deep as infinity, void as a gas,
On which they plant the lying rose
To delude the sniffing child or the fool.
But me they cannot expect

To wink forever, never to turn
And look at their empty stage
Of space starless and planetless
Where they swarm to cover some nakedness,
A ravaged fruit tree perhaps, some sin
That calls to me to judge.

One question has to be wrestled down
Before I smash this façade:
Are they worlds, these other men, Thomas or **Roger**,
Like me, with their plague of conjurers
Or but lesser dolls in the scene of one
Who will deal alone with God?

BEWARE, SAUNTERER, OF THIS
DESPERADO, A MR. BONES, A BAD ACTOR

Saunterer on this autumn track
That edges the garden, brown with brown,
Along by the hickory tree remember
To avoid the place where the dead rat lies.

Else how will you breathe untainted the sweet
Rot of the indolent cucumber,
Apple-smell, stubble-reek, pumpkin-vinegar?

Someone is taking all the parts
In this season's performance—ha! leaping the footlights
Where your beating blood is most gay with his masking,
Marks your time too with his ticking bomb.

A nation of hayricks spotting the green solace
    Of grass,
And thrones of thatch ruling a yellow kingdom
    Of barley.

In the green lands, the white nation of sheep.
    And the woodlands,
Red, the delicate tribes of roebuck, doe
    And fawn.

A senate of steeples guarding the slaty and gabled
    Shires,
While aloof the elder houses hold a secret
    Sceptre.

To the north, a wall touching two stone-grey reaches
    Of water;
A circle of stones; then to the south a chalk-white
    Stallion.

To the north, the wireless towers upon the cliff.
    Southward
The powerhouse, and monstrous constellations
    Of cities.

To the north, the pilgrims along the holy roads
    To Walsingham,
And southward, the road to Shottery, shining
    With daisies.

Over the castle of Warwick frightened birds
    Are fleeing,
And on the bridge, faces upturned to a roaring
    Falcon.

I who am sanctified—
Having lain with the holy harlots at Askelon
On the roof of the great temple under her visage
Who graces with splendor the night in the god-filled sky:
Mother, rich-wombed mistress, whose thighs are forever
Rising and falling like the tides in the roadstead of Gath,
To strike with fear the arid and impotent damned
And assure the fruit of field and man and animal
With Adonis and her chosen, fortunate priests—
Must tell you of these barbarians from the mountains,
From the anarchic hills come to destroy us,
Recent siftings out of the east and south.

They call her the White One or the White Lady
But do not worship her nor any mother-goddess.

I have seen them on the high days in Askelon
When the harlots dance naked through the gala streets
For the joy of Adonis and the blessed thirst of the loins
Turn away angry, cursing these holy bodies,
Crying, "Let them be stoned and their evil wombs ripped
          up."
They hate delight. They have but a lone god
And he is their enemy. I met a certain one:
Sly as a jackal yet arrogant as a lion,
Rough-bearded, out of the desert, desperate
With his private phantoms, his eyes like an animal's
(Fearful, and darting here and there, yet ready
To spring and rend), his hair and garments filthy
With the rot of caves, his skin flayed red by scorpions.
Though his nights are writhings of fire, he will not clasp
The salvation of sweet flesh, but for sustenance

Communes with this impossible imageless demon,
Stuff of a barren race, who has tainted him
With a sickness I cannot fathom, an evil spirit
Like the guilt which dogs a murderer. So always
He looks behind him, before, and within himself,
And the voice he hears becomes this maniacal thundering
On our sunlit streets and before our gleaming temples.

What I saw in the eyes of this vagrant (one of a tribe
Cultureless, without iron, art, or altar)
Was the whole world made somber, and man lonely
In a proud empty heaven like a hell,
Estranged from the field and the beast and his own body
And kin to the mothering earth only in death.
I cannot break this knot, but I know he thought—
And I thought too in the wizardry of that moment—
Our sunwashed cities despicable and meaningless,
Our splendid artistic productions abominable,
Our majestic pantheon foul as a kennel,
The harbor jostling with keen ships and mariners
From the farthest ocean, trivial as a sigh.
And joy unimportant too. The dignity of sorrow
Was the only blessing under the cloud of his god.

I say these are faces of stone no years can weather.
They scheme to take your ease. Listen, you nations:
They will lure you from your spontaneous ecstasies
And positive possessions, and with themselves,
Carry you forth on arduous pilgrimages
Whose only triumph can be a bitter knowledge
Out of the suffering they make our worth.
They see the desert in the growing leaf:

That is their sickness. The sky will be darker then;
The White Lady of splendid thighs and bosom
Without a seedsman or a harvester,
A pallid virgin; and the lands beneath
Dark with this god and people. I who am wise
Through the sacred harlots' embraces know the syllables
(Ah, they are powerful and barbarous!)
Of the secret incantation that gives them strength.
Hear how they thunder! Listen: *Issachar*
Levi simon reuben judah dan
Zebulun asher naphtali menassah ephraim.

I IMAGINED A PAINTER
PAINTING SUCH A WORLD

Like successive layers of leaf that dwindle the sunlight
Are the overlapping cumulative shadows
Projected by things, which huddle in them darkly
Within the greater shadow: suffering.

Breaching the shores of matter a swell of shadows
Destroys all sanctions of formal separateness;
And objects, transposed of vesture, take doubtful values
Like hulks vaguely discerned under the tides.

What inner or outer flames may shine are random
In the one, shadowed sea where all things melt,
While through all, the superior dark, the subjective night
Encloses and bathes the universe.

To whom do the bass pay homage,
Leaping to break the dimness
Of the reedy, dawn-gray water?

I heard the rare message
From Sirius and Capella,
The Dog-Star and the Goat,

Whom I saw as I rode to this water
Over the empty streets
And the houses cold with dream.

They have paled into the sunlight
That whitens the upper air,
But they say still: "Come,

"We are the great fireflies,
Sweeter than soft minnows.
Take us before we fade."

And the shape with the whispering lure,
The dark shape with the net,
Draws them to that shore.

THE IMPORTANCE OF POETRY,
OR THE COMING FORTH
FROM ETERNITY INTO TIME

Beyond the image of the willow
There is a willow no man knows
Or watches with corruptible eyes.

Deep in a field where no man goes
Nor bird flies
The willow fronts an empty road.

The bird hovers in other skies:
World where only these wings exist.

And elsewhere, alone, upon an abyss,
The man is marching down a road.

As the rays of the sun are drawn together
By a curved glass and rekindled to fire
So, to the poppies life and death,
So does desire
Draw them and bend them and bind them so,
So the noise of the wings can at last be heard
And the willow-image do grace to a bird
And the ghost on the roadway give them word
Not for forever, only a day.

The illusion is one of flatness: the sky
Has no depth, is a sheet of tin
Upon which the blackened branches and twigs
Are corroded, burnt in
By a strong acid:

Hang there, outside the squares of pane—
Work of a gruff but extraordinary artist,
Who has done good things in pastels too,
In summer scenes, leaf-stuff
And the placid

Nuances of snow.
Since, as we know,
Genius is superior to praise or blame,
He will not mind if I suggest:
"Fewer cold subjects please (they do not please!).
Really, your leafy stuff, Sir, is best."

If these lesser things are subsumed within the **Good**—
These corrupt shapes: desk, mirror or tree—
The falsely transliterated, strangely planed
Creatures of eyesight and the sentient bones
(Themselves in the web of the spider), then all times
Are poses of the one actor, Time: he
Who is ape of eternity, and the acorn neglected among
        leaves
Encircles, now in this very heartbeat, a forest
Of oaks that have no horizon; and the still white egg
On the tablecloth in the hush of morning is turbulent
With the cackle of a universe of chickens;
And still it is hot noon on the sea Tethys
Where the protoplasmic slime begets Aphrodite
Whose belly is history till the moon falls
And the last spore flames like Andromeda.

You called me a name on such and such a day—
Do you remember?—you were speaking of Bleistein our
       brother,
The barbarian with the black cigar, and the pockets
Ringing with cash, and the eyes seeking Jerusalem,
Knowing they have been tricked. Come, brother Thomas,
We three must weep together for our exile.

I see the hunted look, the protestation,
The desperate seeking, the reticence and the brashness
Of the giver of laws to the worshippers of calves.
At times you speak as if the words were walls,
But your walls fell with mine to the torch of a Titus.
Come, let us weep together for our exile.

We two, no doubt, could accommodate ourselves:
We've both read Dante and we both dislike Chicago,
And both, you see, can be brutal—but you must bow down
To our brother Bleistein here, with the unaesthetic
Cigar and the somber look. Come, do so quickly,
For we must weep together for our exile.

O you may enwomb yourself in words or the Word
(The Word is a good refuge for people too proud
To swallow the milk of the mild Jesus' teaching),
Or a garden in Hampshire with a magic bird, or an old
Quotation from the Reverend Andrewes, yet someone or
       something
(Let us pause to weep together for our exile)

Will stick a needle in your balloon, Thomas.
Is it the shape that you saw upon the stair?
The four knights clanking toward the altar? the hidden

Card in the deck? the sinister man from Nippon?
The hordes on the eastern horizon? Come, brother Bur-
    bank,
And let us weep together for our exile.

In the time of sweet sighing you wept bitterly,
And now in the time of weeping you cannot weep.
Will you wait for the peace of the sailor with pearly
    bones?
Where is the refuge you thought you would find on the
    island
Where each man lives in his castle? O brother Thomas,
Come let us weep together for our exile.

You drew us first by your scorn, first by your wit;
Later for your own eloquent suffering.
We loved you first for the wicked things you wrote
Of those you acknowledged infinitely gentle.
Wit is the sin that you must expiate.
Bow down to them, and let us weep for our exile.

I see your words wrung out in pain, but never
The true compassion for creatures with you, that Dante
Knew in his nine hells. O eagle! master!
The eagle's ways of pride and scorn will not save
Though the voice cries loud in humility. Thomas, Thomas,
Come, let us pray together for our exile.

You, hypocrite lecteur! mon semblable! mon frère!

A NEW EXPLANATION OF THE QUIETUDE AND TALKATIVENESS OF TREES

Because they belong to the genus thunder
Trees grow still when their patriarch
Delivers his sign, the livid spark,
And comes himself with a rumble and mutter,

Reminding them of their dignity.
Boom! He empties a bucket of wet
Across their shoulders, but they submit
Till he huffs away. So they are free

With a stirring of limbs to echo him,
A confab of whispers, a hushing and mumming,
Till time comes round again for the thrumming
Harumph of the father to quiet them.

PORTRAIT

Notice with what careful nonchalance
He tries to be a Jew casually,
To ignore the monster, the mountain—
A few thousand years of history.

Of course he personally remembers nothing,
And the world has forgotten the older objections—
The new ones not being socially acceptable:
Hangdogs, hiding in the privies and alleys of the mind.

It is agreed
That he of all men has gained the right to his soul
(Though like the others he no longer believes in one).
He lives in his own house under his oak.
He stands by his car, shod in decently-grained leather.
He is smiling. His hair is peacefully in place.
His suit is carefully pressed; his cravat harmonious.

Whose father, it is whispered, stubbornly cried old clothes
          and bric-a-brac,
He of all men might yet be master of self, all self-
          possession,
Were it not (how gauche and incredible!) for the one ill-
          fitting garment—
The historical oversight in the antique wardrobe—
The shirt, the borrowed shirt,
The Greek shirt.

Notice how even when at ease he is somehow anxious,
Like a horse who whiffs smoke somewhere nearby faintly.
Notice with what nonchalance,
The magazine in his hand and the casual cigarette to his
          lips,
He wears a shirt by Nessus.

[*31*]

The sudden translation to the bottom of the hill,
To be with the dull stones and the sterile earth
After the bitter climbing of forty-four years.

You who postponed the quiet amenities,
The lazy conversation after lunch,
The cigarette in mid-afternoon, the daydream
When a certain wind came to your window
Out of that young, beautiful sea, the Atlantic.

Night. Nighttime in the earth.
The body settles patiently into eternity.
Time moves, yes, but like glacial ice.
The tireless eyes stare out of the sky, answering nothing,
And the silence is august and terrible.

While we were lost in our petty commerce
Of coming and going (that day a barking dog annoyed us,
A buzzing insect, a lagging clock)
You suddenly left your house, your city and your country,
Traveling in the night, few knowing,
To fight with a dark archangel in a desert.

Already there is no one to call to.
The body of Edward is not Edward,
Nor the ashes of Gregory Gregory.
Alexander is no longer Alexander in the earth.

Nothing can be done but something can be said at least.

AND IN THE 51ST YEAR OF THAT CENTURY,
WHILE MY BROTHER CRIED IN THE TRENCH,
WHILE MY ENEMY GLARED FROM THE CAVE

This star is only an augury of the morning,
Gift-bearer of another day.

A wind has brought the musk of thirty fields,
Each like a coin of silver under that sky.

Precious, the soundless breathing of wife and children
In a house on a field lit by the morning star.

Having won through, you and I regard each other
Remembering in our bones the interminable snow and the
        ache of an iron frost,
You with your buds like velvet, tasting the atmosphere
Which I too breathe, incredulous and lustful,
And I, desperate to halt a running moment,
Casting lariats of nothing at an arch and graceful fawn.

When your leaves are the size of a mouse's ears, they say,
The trout hunger for self-destruction.
Ah, time is the fawn that comes down to those waters.
They see her eyes as she drinks, and leap to her.
How silent she flits now below your branches,
Being already in tomorrow.

When your leaves grow to the size of a fox's ears
She will be in the field with the fox and mouse.
A haunter of the margins of forests, she will be seen
By the man driving a fine team of horses
And those who pass by in cars in midsummer.
But no one will pause, for they have no time.
She cannot reach your leaves, but she will return
When they are ready to fall to her.
Her feet will rustle among them, and I shall be waiting.
But she will already be in yesterday.

OF OBJECTS CONSIDERED
AS FORTRESSES IN A BALEFUL SPACE

I and the other intruders,
The oak and stone my brothers,
Stare at one another
Upon the plain of nothing.

As if to ask what wonder
By willing or by blunder
Could lead to this encounter
Upon the plain of nothing.

(As if to ask what meeting
Could overmatch the wonder
Of opaque hostile Being
Emergent out of nothing.)

The nothing is a glitter
Wicked, a frosty water,
Upon which no words scatter,
Not hallo, sob or laughter.

Upon their petty islands
The something and the something,
Knowing or blank, in silence
Await the will of nothing.

One, one, and one,
Mysteries of the moon,
And the always never-guests,
None, none.

A PHILOSOPHER ON A MOUNTAIN
IN SCYTHIA

We shall come back at last to the Lord Snow
After the Lord Fire is quenched at last.

His gray, antique mantle will cover neatly
The eyeballs' nightmare of hue and diversity.

White will be black when the Lord Snow is master,
Under his coat completing the last reduction.

Lord, the wound that the Lord Fire branded
Hot as a heart, deep as seventy years,

Heal, the touch of whose mild fingers is peace.

A vista of vague flakes like a framed star-field
Falling in unison to unity.

TRIO FOR TWO VOICES AND A
WOODWIND

You for whom the waters of no spring are sweet:
Consider, in their respective empires, vegetal and animal,
Men and trees, bearers of the sceptre.

Laughing, our leafy Caesar might shrug,
"A pusillanimous cousin!" (as we would refer
To a ring-tailed monkey or an indiscreet baboon)—
Or, "an oversized, ambulatory mandrake,"
Or better, "a carrot, defective, cloven."

Man, however, must sooner or later lecture:
"A tree is a river system,
Continental, a lovely schema against a background
Of sky brightness and earth green and brownness:
Tiny dark runnels, myriad yet distinct, starting up there
        in the light,
Becoming rivulets, always traveling inward as if drawn
        by hunger,
Becoming brooks, creeks, tributary rivers,
And the one great river flowing into a planet.
The tree is the antecedent symbolism.
A man must always be part of the tree of the living;
A tree, of no man, of itself only.
What, tell me, feeds on pure air and energy?
And what, as in the beginning, on the bitter fruit of a
        tree?"

Excellently done, Professor.—
And you whose tears drip poison into the well:
No longer will you be restless when the belief they offer
        you—

As, under the very noses of the archangels,
The oldest story has secretly winked it—
Has a tree as its god or prophet.
The animals with nimble forefeet, hitherto the only vol-
uble observers,
Have long been biased.
There are no bears, swans or heroes among the constella-
tions—
Only, throughout all space, branches budded with fire,
From which, in an ether where never a wind shivers,
Sift and sink the burning flower-flakes of time
(Breathgiver, incendiary, refiner of the sorrowful metal
That rises, walks and sings like a man;
Whitener, when the flakes are ashes,
Of philosophical skulls in a valley.)

THE MYTHOS OF THE MAN FROM ENOCH

Faintly against the stars,
From the northmost march to the Crab,
I see the undulant outlines
Of the vast, ameboid Spirit.

Foggy grains of fire
Light the tortuous paths
Within the hungry hands,
Brain, body and feet.

Time is already victim
And at only the farthest milestone
Is there space pure as water
Upon a delectable mountain.

I cannot reach those ranges.
Hours become a lifetime
As I linger at each crossroads
Waiting the blow on the cheek.

God is brutish life!
God is the living ether!
Within these strange entrails
We must build our beautiful houses.

The milkman walks with mysterious movements,
Translating will to energy—
To the crunch of his feet on crystalline water—
While the bad angels mutter.

A white ghost in an opaque body
Passing slowly over the snow,
And a telltale fume on the frozen air
To spite the princes of terror.

One night they will knock on the milkman's door,
Their boots crunch hard on the front-porch floor.
One-two, open the door.

You are the thief of the secret flame,
The forbidden bread, the terrible Name.
Return what is left; go back where you came.

One-two, the slam of a door.
A woman crying: Who is there?
And voices mumbling beyond the stair.

Is there a fume in the frozen sky
To spell that someone has been by,
Under the sun and over the snow?

THE LAST FISHERMAN

He will set his camp beside a cold lake
And when the great fish leap to his lure, shout high
To three crows battling a northern wind.

Now when the barren twilight closes its circle
Will fear the yearning ghosts come for his catch
And watch intently trees move in the dark.

Fear as the last fire cringes and sputters,
Heap the branches, strike the reluctant ashes,
Lie down restless, rise when the dawn grays.

Time runs out as the hook lashes the water
Day after day, and as the days wane
Wait still for the wonder.

THE SHEPHERD
(*from* "Horatio")

[*Horatio has spent his life defending the memory of
Hamlet, the friend of his youth. Now an old man, he sits
in his study and writes of his latest experience.*]

Even if time permits me further breath
Beyond these fading four and eighty years,
This is the last circuit of my lands.
The roads are harsh to an old body. It is simpler
To listen to a strong-eyed servant reading
A letter brought by a brawny courier
Whose arm will not shake though he lifts our heaviest
       tankard
Full to the brim, into the river of sun
That pours through the eastern window of our kitchens,
And then, with a loud chuckle, gulps her down.
I have been thinking of a smaller drink—
One sip of a strong poison, I might have drunk.
Among the eternal torments prepared for such
In the infamous pit, one at least would be lacking
(Whispering like the fiend, morning and evening):
"If Moses is dead, how then will Aaron speak?"

From Bern, bailiff of my farthest seignory
(This promontory, the desolate uttermost horn
Of Danish ground, goading the mad Baltic)
Two days ago, in casual talk, I heard
Of confused tales told in this district,
By hill shepherds, touching Hamlet my friend.
We went together, mounted at first, and then
Our horses left behind in a hidden gully,

Afoot the final hours, hearing once
The howl of a wolf, so up a craggy incline,
Climbing into a range of rock-gnarled grassland
Not far from the sea. There, playing at homeless beggars,
Father and son, our clothes well-picked for the part,
We came at the time of the first star to a campfire
Where, at the mouth of a cave, some shepherds waited
While one of their number tended a spitted lamb
Whose fragrance tingled the air. We ate and drank
And I fell asleep. The hand of Bern the bailiff
Shook hard my shoulder. I opened my eyes. The constel-
lations
Hung huge in their vastness. An urgent, small, cracked
voice,
Garrulous, croaked a crooked track through the silence
About a hero, a dragon, a prince's daughter,
And suchlike nonsense. Propped upon an elbow
I saw that I was one of a listening circle
Of ten or a dozen shadows, around an ember
(The remains of a campfire) that gleamed like a sly
Cyclops.

One said: "Did you hear him? The wolf's been talking
again.
And the Bear is keener and huger tonight than ever
Up in the sky, and his cousins the weasel and fox,
Whipped by the smell of our meat, rustle the grass.
See that gleam by the bush. Pile on a log.
(May our dogs with the aid of God guard well our fold.)
And down below, the sea-surf's been furious.
So give us the tale of the madman."

And the story-teller
Cackling: "Ah, he gnashes his teeth on the rocks!"

"Who?" I cried.

                "Is grandfather then awake?
Good. Why, that devil, the prince Ambleth of course.
He grinds his teeth on the shore to make the flour
(Or so they say, ha ha!) to fill his stomach.
Give me a leg of that meat. Ah, good, in faith!—

"Listen. In the sorrowful time of the old dusk
Before the sun of Christ gave light to the world
There lived in Denmark two brothers, Fang and Hunger.
Hunger was king but Fang envied his place,
And desired too, being lusty, the Queen Gertha
Because of her yellow hair and her green eyes
(This was like barley, those the hue of the sea).
Now once, while Hunger was gone to fight the Polack,
Fang to Gertha acknowledged his fierce lust
And found it returned, so that, while Hunger was absent
They lay together often in the royal bedchamber
To which Fang could come by a secret door, known only
To a mum and snickering cuckquean of the Queen's,
A witch with a squinty face. But soon thereafter,
Yet following duly Hunger's return from the war,
So none suspected the mischief between the sheets,
Gertha grew big in the belly with a son,
Who, when the time was come, to the banging of bells,
The shooting of cannon and the ringing of numerous
        flagons,
Was named Prince Ambleth, and who, as the years went
        on,

Grew up to manhood. Meanwhile Fang and the Queen,
Whenever occasion offered, resumed their embraces;
And meanwhile Fang waited for Hunger's death
Patiently, year after year, praying to Satan
The god of the country. Often he thought to kill him
By a knife, a dagger, poison poured in his soup,
A twisted rope, an arrow from the green wood,
Or the hands of a hired strangler (who could be silenced)
But always he drew back. But when Hunger suddenly,
Breathing the grace of God from a wandering priest,
Gave up his demons and the abominable mysteries
Of worship under the oak (that our wise men tell us
Our fathers practised), and acknowledged the sweetness
          of Christ
And changing his foul name (named for a devil
Who lives in a gut) called himself, meekly, Humble,
And converted his people also—then could Fang
Endure it no longer, but with the aid of the Queen
And an old and crafty courtier, Polonio,
He plotted his brother's death. They came upon Humble
Once as he sat in an arbor within his garden
Toward evening, dreaming of good. Three times they
          touched him,
While the great cape of Polonio covered his face
And throttled his cries, with delicate poisoned daggers
That drew no blood, and would have left him lying
(Having already spread a careful rumor
Of a poison adder seen underneath the building)
To be found by a servant, and the news so spread abroad.
But Fang when he stood above his enemy dead
(Polonio and the Queen having fled at once)
In terrible rage slashed at the helpless corpse

And when he saw the blood, grew desperate,
Dragged off the body in secret, quartered it,
And threw the shaking parts into the sewer
Which quickly bore them down to the sea. And there
A wolf, a fox, a weasel, a fish and an eagle,
Magical creatures of Fang, already waited—
Attracted by his powerful thought—and snatched
Each a portion of Humble's ruined body
And fled, each to his hole, or eyrie, or cavern
To hide his loot. So Fang now ruled as King
While Humble, report said, had been taken away
By a powerful oaken god whom he had dishonored
And who now returned for worship—'which he would re-
      ceive
From the newly crowned King, Fang the Gentle,
And his new-wed queen, Gertha. All-hail to Satan!' "

The shepherd crossed himself. The fire winked.
The sea screamed on the beach.

              "But listen, my brothers.
On a certain midnight, Prince Ambleth, walking the ram-
      parts
With a bosom friend, Honorio, sleepless in grief
For the man he thought his father, suddenly saw
The woebegone ghost of this Humble, who, wailing, cried
      out:

" 'My son Ambleth, strike down your father's murderer!'

"And Ambleth: 'Ah, is it so? Tell me his name
And I shall darken his eyes within this hour,
As the Lord God Omnipotent is my witness,
Whether he be in Denmark, Thule, or Hell!'

"And the ghost, quietly: 'Seek but in Denmark and Thule.
As for the other, do you not see the ash
That darkens my ghostly gown? The name of my mur-
          derer
I do not know, my son. Asleep in my arbor
I woke to this deeper sleep with a cloak or cloth
Over my face, while the steel bit deep in my body.
But I thought in that slight moment before my spirit
Was rapt away and set by the far-off wicket
With shadowy others in judgment, I thought I heard
The hoarse, muttered curse of my brother Fang.
Ah, but beware you kill an innocent man,
Else I will have the sin of Cain on my head
To drag me further downward into the pit—
And you a like damnation. Be certain, then strike.
Thereafter gather together the torn pieces
Of my earthly body, that five strange animals—
A wolf, a fox, a weasel, a fish and an eagle—
Have hidden within their hole or eyrie or cavern
And bury me with the fit Christian rites
If you would have my torments below endurable
And my arm strong for a battle that I must fight
Upon the flame-tipped grass of the spiritual plain,
Soon or late, in the shadow the future watches . . .'

"So Ambleth swore revenge and burial
And so, after that night in the court and street,
Distracted, numb, with red-shot, half-closed eyes
He stared into people's faces, seeking a secret—
And most at Fang, who in turn quickly suspecting
Ambleth's suspicion, would, sitting upon his throne
Turn on the prince in the midst of official affairs

[47]

A lingering halting glance, while his nostrils quivered
As he whiffed the smell of danger. This, Ambleth saw
And fearing the stifling cloth over his face
And the stab in the dark, which King Humble got, de-
        cided
That the game of madness would suit him best. He wiped
Snivel and smut on his features, wore a purple mitten
Or a chamberpot for a hat, and sometimes while singing
A lullaby or reciting tick-tack-toe
Would piss from an upper chamber of the castle
Upon the unfortunate dogs and cats of the place—"

As the speaker paused, a whinnying laugh arose
From the shadowy circle, and from time to time was re-
        sumed.

"But Fang, uneasy, still not wholly certain
If the Prince Ambleth's madness was real or feigned
Decided to test him, and advised thereto by his cronies
Lured our Ambleth one night down to the beach
Where a certain wench, Olivia, willing and able,
Waited for him. To the spies, if he lay with her
That would be witness his mind was sane enough
To know a right good thing when it came his way,
Whereas if he should spurn the fine occasion
He'd be as crazy as any man yet was—"

A snicker rose beyond the fire.

                                    "But Ambleth,
Just as he prepared to do the trick,
Was warned by his cunning friend, Honorio,
By means of a firefly with a painted straw

Stuck up its arse, that something was amiss.
Quickly with violent strength he dragged Olivia,
Avoiding pursuers, into the heavy wood
Where, in fear, she broke away. Meanwhile the Queen,
Catching a hint of some plot that touched her son
And afraid for his life, rushed, all desperate
Down to the shore, blundering and crying
In the maze of trees, rocks and cruel brambles
Where Ambleth sought Olivia. In the utter dark,
While the raging ocean below covered all sound,
Ambleth seized his mother and ravished her
(Unknowing, of course) and, done with this nameless deed,
Clapped in her hand a golden medallion
That he ripped from around his neck, and howled in her
            ear
Over a lucky lull of the roaring waves:

" 'Here are your wages, whore! which ought to keep you
Till you frolic with someone else tomorrow night.
Say nothing, or I will arrange to have you locked
In that nunnery, Earth, where there's no more tumbling
            and tossing.
Do you understand?'

                "He stumbled away in the dark
And soon was lost among tree-trunks, bushes and boulders.
Once he fell in a thorn-filled ditch, and once
Preparing to take a step he saw of a sudden
Before his feet, reflecting the cold ray
Of a rotting log, a pool which went from him
Into the darkness as if it meant to reach
The end of the world. He turned, and watched affrighted

Two burning eyes, green as a cat's, appearing
And disappearing, as if approaching him
Down by the water—and of a height, seemingly,
To indicate some beast. With his two arms,
Turning he grasped a tree that rose beside him
So large in size he could not circle it,
But the shaggy bark gave him handhold and foothold
And grunting a broken oath he clambered up
To a low branch, where, sitting breathless a while,
He thought he heard in another lull of the surf
A muttering voice somewhere below. With care
And feeling his way, he unexpectedly found
A safe, broad, comfortable perch, where he lay back pant-
     ing . . .

"He opened his eyes. The air glittered like gold
While huge from the quarter sky into his face
A full moon shone, and as he watched, a spot
Darkened its disk, grew larger, became at last
A great black bird flying toward him
With outstretched wings, till the whole planet was cov-
     ered,
Yet the strong light from behind outlined the bird.
At last, as the upper edge of the moon reappeared,
One instant within it a cruel beak was limned
And the disk was clear again. In the opposite sky
A faintness hinted that night was nearing its end.
Among the trees, the silent ocean shone.
Where was the surf? Had the tide then reached its full?
He turned in his place and over the edge of his branch
Looked down at the dark pool of his night's adventure,
As it lay in the moonlight, calm and deep and wide.

A sudden gigantic fin thrust through the surface
And sank, and the water writhed a little after.
He heard a muttering voice, and there below him,
In a smooth moondrenched clearing among the tree-
        trunks,
A red roebuck with ripped throat and sides
Lay on the ground. Nearby a fox sat grinning,
Sniffed, and said with an impatient whine:

" 'Where are they then? I will not wait much longer.
By Magog! there is enough for all—'

                         " 'Be patient
Or you'll regret it!' whistled a beast, a weasel
Till then unnoticed, down by the water's edge,
Whose fur glistened sleek like a wet stone.

"The fox went up and hungrily nuzzled the deer
But turned at an unheard hint from the forest. A wolf,
Huge and gray and with head held high, entered
And looked behind him. To a battering of wings
An eagle swooped from the upper dark, whose eyes
Followed the gaze of the wolf, the fox and the weasel,
And the look too of the fish, who had silently thrust
His snout from the water, and watched with bulging eye-
        balls.
Out of the dark, Fang came forward scowling,
Bowed and was bowed to. Together, making a circle
Around the bleeding deer, they lifted their heads
In a low, howling prayer to some fiend,
Then fell to the feast with beak and claw and hand—
With due morsels thrown to the maw in the pool—
Till the feast was done and the platter clean as grass.

"At which King Fang, wiping his mouth, laughed:
'He suspects nothing, being so bedlam mad
That even the prickings of lust leave him untouched.
The castle whispers with laughter at this simpleton
Who dragged a willing leman into the woods—
For what? To gambol about in some childish game.
(All this she told us.) So I am safe, my sons,
To empty this scabbard for building of the age
(Already begun, foretold in the prophecies)
Of whoredom, the axe and the sword, the wind and the
          wolf.
Keep well your charge; hell only knows what tricks
He may try there in the dubious place where he thirsts
For that sacrament, that holy water, to quench
The heat that makes him unquiet, the little flame
That keeps him from perfection; what emissaries,
Whether from there or here, and of sly strength
Or wearing the form of weakness, he may send
To lure you away from your watch, or, when you falter,
Pierce you with his steel. In my days of breath,
His body unsanctified and separate
Within the powerful keeping of each of you
Renders him helpless as a wisp of vapor
To stand athwart my business. And at my dying,
In the continuing struggle through eternity
So much, my brothers, as the parts of his ruined form
Are divided and unblest, so far I win.
And in the final encounter face to face—
The occasion is certain, the outcome unknown, the time
Nameless, soon or late—in the last meeting,
With all to gain or lose in a single thrust,
Some of his strength must still be in your keeping

If you would not have his brightness blind my eyes
And confuse my hand. Yet if he should press me still,
Could I not sweetly murmur into his ear
A secret about himself, or of some he thought
Part of himself, that would shake his arm and shield?
Go now. Relieve your henchmen, and do not sleep.'

"They went away: the fox, the weasel, the wolf.
The eagle flew off, the fish sank in the pool.
And as Fang stood there a moment in thought, Am-
          bleth
Leaped from the tree shouting; most skilfully
Lit on the springy earth; fell; rose
And grappled with Fang, who had turned in alarm
Unable to draw his sword—they were so close together
(Ambleth himself having no weapon at all).
They toppled, their hands reached for the throat of each
          other.
A savage tussle, and they lay for a long time quiet,
A long long time, then one of them shaking stood up
And saw the aimless limbs of the man he had strangled
And the wide eyes, and heard nearby a sighing,
Small, faint, like a muffled sob, which came
(He was sure it had been in his ears a long time back)
From the pool, where the head of the great fish was
          straining
Against the shore, and the round inhuman eyes
Stared without meaning. Bracing his feet in haste
He heaved the dead man up by his hair and beard
And whirling around as if he wielded a scythe
Flung him from him into the dark water,
Where he sank, and the evil maw of the fish also.

And the water was quiet. The sword in its jeweled scab-
        bard,
Undone in the fighting, lay on the ground.
He buckled it on, and drawing the weapon high
Ran through the trees in the dew-wet paths of dawn
Toward the crowing of cocks. From a leaning boulder
That troubled his path a shape leaped for his face.
He ducked and, fading sideways, slashed with his sword,
And the weasel lay on the ground, his open mouth
Asking no mercy as his life-blood throbbed away.
A hurried yapping came from somewhere behind,
And a howling that ever grew louder; he came to the high-
        road;
Knew his position; ran past the creaking wagons
Of farmers going to market; arrived at last
At the Castle Elsinore, where the guards, in astonishment,
Saluted and gave him entrance. Past frightened courtiers
He ran to the Queen's apartments, beat on the door
With his sword still bloody, and wrenching open the knob
Entered. The Queen sat in her chair by the fire
Attended by a maid, a squinting witch,
Whom he ordered out with a look, which the Queen
        seconded.

"She spoke in a low voice but her eyes were screaming.
'What do you want, Ambleth, my son?'

                          "And Ambleth,
Husky, intense, 'I have killed the murderer.'

" 'Who? Of whom?'

                    " 'Fang, who murdered my father . . .'

"And her eyes grew glazed in her bruised face, and the
           scream
Entered her mouth and: 'Fool! Fang was your father!
Him I lay with on the night you were conceived—
And often before and after . . .'

                    "Ambleth stood rooted,
His weapon frozen in air. And: 'Why do you wait,
Since your sword is out?—'

                    "Ambleth's arm dropped down.
She leaned forward and grasped the arms of her chair.

" 'Fang was your father, and Humble was a cuckold,
And I—I was with Fang when we threw the cloak
Over his sleeping face, to stifle his cries
While we stabbed him . . .'

                    "She rose, and Ambleth backed away.
And quietly, as her hand came up from the table:
'Oh, since you turn to leave, better take this.
If you should choose, perchance, to amuse yourself
Tonight with some woman, you might give her this as a
           wage.
Warn her, of course, to say nothing, lest you might
           arrange
To have her locked in that gentle nunnery, Earth,
Where there's no more tumbling and tossing.'

                    "She let the medallion
Drop to the floor, and with bruised cheek averted
Whipped up the little dagger from the table,
Thrust deep, and fell. And Ambleth cried aloud.
But the clock on the wall ticked louder than his cry

And the hands whirled like the spokes of a wheel. He ran
Through the halls of Elsinore screaming—and screaming,
     down
To the sad ocean, where he felt the tides heaving,
While overhead the sun whisked through the sky
Light as a child's ball. He saw, looking behind,
The wood and the world, where the fox and the wolf still
     hid
And, somewhere, the den of the weasel without a bar.
A tower of seven heavens hung on his head
Within which a proud bird could track and hide.
But the mountains were settling and crumbling, and his
     heart tolled
Loud as the clock in his dead mother's chamber.
Holding at ready the weapon of Fang, he strode
With eyes open into the dark waves."

And the story-teller, listening, leaned forward
To the firelit faces bent toward the sea.

"He gnashes his teeth on the shore when the quest grows
     desperate,
Would gulp the ocean, curl his lips round the world,
Swallow the sky, to still the maddening multitude
Of hounds and crickets, with their round whirling faces
That creak and tick and yell from each blade of grass,
Each drop of the sea, sand-grain, or bubble of air,
Beast and fish and man and tree. Sometimes,
Seeing the sun wane in the hand of God
He flings himself toward the Evening Star
Or prowls the abysses behind the throne of Saturn.
Once at heaven's gate near the house of the Unicorn

He found, new-wet with blood, a small bird's feathers
And heard the whirring of cruel wings, but the night
Confused his search and he sank down weeping
Into the sea."

      The voice faded and lapsed
And a hissing stick in the fire filled the silence.

The sea was silent when the cackling voice concluded.
Soon after, I and my bailiff took our leave,
For the dawn was coming. We followed our old path,
Retrieved our horses, and with hardly a word to each other
Returned to this castle Forstness where I write.
If I thought at all, it was only to dwell slightly
On the story-teller's later question: "Old man,
What do you say to our tale?"

        While Bern watched me
With a small smile, I whispered something at last:
"Do you recall that your Ambleth had a friend,
Honorio, with whom he saw the ghost,
And who, as you tell it, warned him of the trap
Set by the King—well, *I* was this Honorio . . ."

They fell into an ecstasy of laughter.

And another said, poking a stick in the fire:
"There is one point that has ever puzzled me
About this tale. How is it that the madman,
When treed over the pool, was not detected
By the beasts below? A weasel's got a nose
Can whiff a fat goose at a hundred furlongs,
With the wind at his back, I'll vouch."

[57]

And said another:
"What of Reynard? He can smell his lady in heat
At ten mile."

"Ho ho!" another chimed.
"So Ambleth smelled like a vixen or a bitch?
I thought there was something odd about the fellow."

"And what of an eagle?" another interposed.
"Though he hangs up there no bigger than a dot
He can smell you out the mole beneath the leaf—"

"He *sees* 'em!" another answered. "His eyes are keener
Than a bailiff's or a—"

"How comes it then
He failed, as he flew by, to see Ambleth?"

"And what of the fish? Fishes can smell—"

"Not so!"

The old man raised his hand. "Hush now, my sons.
These were, remember, magical animals
Whose senses differ—"

"And what of the crickets and dogs?
I had a lively bitch one time that barked
With the very chirp of a cricket—"

"Bah, *you* chirp
Like a cricket yourself . . ."

We left them grumbling there
While I, on the final lap, resumed the words
Which I write here in the study at Forstness, after
The earlier parts of the story written down
In these past years, as the heart makes its summation,
With a lucky mind to help that forgets nothing
Of faces and voices at least—and too much of words.